PREFACE

The pursuit of a Christian view of war which occupies these pages will follow a rather personal course. It reproduces a debate which has taken place in my own mind over a few years, in which I have been protagonist, not for one or the other, but for both sides. I began with a sense, which arose from the demands of teaching, that the case for Christian Pacifism was not usually made in a way that could confront the Just War theory in the form that I had learned from the writings of Paul Ramsey and that I myself held.[1] I began to wonder how such a case for pacifism could be argued, and (such was the power of a train of thought) nearly succeeded in convincing myself of it. Why in the end I have held back will, I hope, be clear from what follows. And, more importantly, I hope it will also be clear that differing Christian views of war, pacifist and non-pacifist, have more in common than is often supposed.

Necessarily this approach to the question is selective. There are a number of different philosophies which may claim the epithet 'pacifist', and different recommendations may spring from them. For the purpose of this discussion, 'pacifism' is the thesis that war is always wrong. I appreciate that not every pacifist would want to frame his belief in these terms: some would say that participation in war is wrong for themselves, as individuals or as Christians, but not necessarily for others; some would believe that in the event of war they ought to share their nation's common guilt at arms; some would believe that in exceptional circumstances the justified war might arise, but for all practical purposes the possibility has to be discounted. To review all the possible options lies beyond the scope of this exercise.

I am inclined to apologise, on behalf of all who write on war without having known it at first hand, to those for whom the subject holds bitter memories. There is, perhaps, a suggestion of impudence in the attempt to discuss such a matter without experience of it. Yet, though we live in peace, the traffic of war always rumbles around the perimeter of our park, and it would be more impudent to ignore the subject than to treat it, as we must, inadequately. Our post-war generation owes to its elders a serious effort to comprehend imaginatively the emotional enormity of what it discusses. Perhaps the poets will serve us best:

> She in the hurling night
> With lucid simple hands
> Stroked away his fright
> Loosed his bloodstained bands
> And seriously aware
> Of the terror she caressed
> Drew his matted hair
> Gladly to her breast.
>
> And he who babbled Death
> Shivered and grew still . . .[2]

Yet even such an effort does not yield any automatic conclusions. It could be said that the poets of the First World War isolated war as a monstrosity without parallel, while their successors in the Second, with no less feeling and compassion, analysed the phenomenon into its constituent experiences of love and death, looking through it as a window onto the general plight of humanity. Something of the same difference of perspective lies behind the debate between pacifism and the Just War.

1 Paul Ramsey, *War and the Christian Conscience* (Duke University Press, Durham, N.C., 1961); *The Just War* (Scribner, New York, 1968).
2 Alun Lewis, 'Compassion', from *Ha! Ha! Among the Trumpets,* (Allen & Unwin, London, 1945).

1. GOVERNMENT AND WAR: THE ANALOGY

'I have often thought to myself how it would have been if, when I served in the first world war, I and some young German had killed each other simultaneously and found ourselves together a moment after death. I cannot imagine that either of us would have felt any resentment or even any embarrassment. I think we might have laughed over it.'[1]

I disliked these words when I first read them, and dislike them still; but it has been a puzzle to tell why. They seem somehow heartless. Is it their support for killing in war that gives offence? Other arguments to the same purpose do not strike me in the same way. Is it the thought that old enemies could laugh and make friends? A Christian could hardly object to that. No, I think it is the lack of embarrassment, or of something rather stronger than embarrassment, at the fact of killing. We would expect at least a *frisson* of horror at the thought that one had killed a man. To have taken a human life, so sacred and serious a thing before God, should make even a spirit feel appalled, and that irrespective of his views on the ethics of war. A soldier serving in Northern Ireland, recounting how he had shot a terrorist marksman, commented: *'That's* something to have on your conscience, isn't it?' From which we might suppose that he was in some moral doubt about what he had done; but we would be wrong. The 'bad conscience' could live alongside the conviction that he had done right, but it showed that he had done it humanely, aware of what his action meant.[2] '"The wise man" they say "will fight just wars". More likely he will break his heart over the *need* for just wars, if he remembers he is a man!'[3]

It is certainly paradoxical, this idea that fighting is a duty which can only be done with a shudder. So difficult is it to grasp, that theological and popular opinion have both tended to divide in two ways to avoid it. On the one hand are those who treat the shudder as decisive, on the other those who suppress it. The traditional 'pacifist', well aware that killing has this effect on us (and if it does not, that only shows our want of higher feelings), concludes that killing cannot possibly be right. To him the shudder is the testimony of the natural conscience, heightened in the Christian by his belief that love is the greatest, and the second greatest, command in the law (Mk. 12.28-34). The Christian 'realist', on the other hand, aware of his duty to a community which may need defence by force or by the threat of it, regards this sense of duty, equally self-evidently, as the demand of the natural conscience. The private virtues of patience and suffering, which are all that the pacifist can recommend, do not satisfy his sense of obligation. But since he too believes that all commands are summed up in the one command, he concludes that fighting, in certain circumstances, is an expression of love for the neighbour. He dismisses any scruples as weakness and irresolution. Since he ought to fight, he ought to fight cheerfully, and when he wins he ought to be pleased and grateful to God. And so the pendulum has swung to and fro in the course of Christian history, back, in our own day, to the militant fervour of Liberation Theology.

1 C. S. Lewis, *Mere Christianity* (Bles, London, 1952), p.94.
2 This is 'conscience' in the emotive, Freudian sense of the term, rather than the rational conscience of St. Thomas Aquinas.
3 St. Augustine, of course, at his most sensitive: *City of God* XIX. 7.

In Pursuit

of a

Christian View

of War

By

Oliver O'Donovan

Tutor at Wycliffe Hall, Oxford

GROVE BOOKS

CONTENTS

Copyright Oliver O'Donovan 1977

First Impression January 1977

ISSN 0305 4241
ISBN 0 905422 04 X

Christianity's divided mind with regard to fighting in war has an interesting and important parallel: the question of responsibility for civil order. Here too there are 'terrible duties' to be performed. Saint Augustine wrote very movingly about the problems facing a conscientious judge who had to administer justice in the brutal conditions of the late Roman Empire, recoiling in horror from what he must do, yet compelled by a sense of public duty to do it.[1] Such anguish is not only for sensitive men in barbarous societies. Anyone who decides to send a man to prison must feel a pang, however right the decision may be, or else he has been brutalized. Augustine would have us see such acts of judicial authority in two lights: the same deed is at once inhuman and terrible, and it is an expression of love. Again subsequent Christian thinking has shrunk from the paradox, so that acts of the magistrate have seemed either unproblematic, love-of-God-and-neighbour *sans phrase,* (so Saint Thomas, Calvin, and the realist majority tradition), or, (as in the sectarian Protestant groups, following a hint in Luther), morally objectionable, threads in a violent social tapestry which the Christian may do nothing to weave.[2]

There is more to this comparison of soldier and magistrate than the un-interesting fact that they both have unpleasant duties. These duties are not simply unpleasant (as, for example, those of an undertaker might be), but run counter to every idea in a Christian's head about the attitudes men should have to one another. The problem, we may say, is the problem of *power.* By gun or by process of law, the soldier and the magistrate exercise power over other men's destinies. They exercise it, not, as a friend might, by invitation and with consent, but in the face of violent resistance or sullen reluctance. Worse, they know perfectly well that they are not acting in their victim's own interests, but are making him suffer in the interests of others. It is not true, as various forms of totalitarianism have maintained, that what is in the interests of all is in the interests of each. It is not true, as the 'social contract' myth maintains, that when the state acts against a member it does so at his implicit invitation. Agents of the state have the duty to do real harm to individuals who really do object. That is what we admit when we reply, 'But they *deserve* it!' for if it were not real harm, or if they really did not mind, questions of desert would not arise. But the Christian's Gospel tells him that victorious relationships come through renouncing power and accepting suffering, not through seeking power and making others suffer. It has taught him to build and not to destroy, to respect and not to override. How, then, can the duties of the soldier and the magistrate ever live with the believer's response to the Gospel of Christ? The tasks of coercion have a strangely unfitting look beside the requirements of the evangelical calling.

---

1 *City of God* XIX.6.

2 This grouping of Luther apart from the realist tradition departs from the conventiona representation, based on his attitude to the Peasants' Revolt. But however tough-minded Luther may have been in practice, the Two Kingdoms theory, by classing the duties of coercion under 'the kingdom of God's left hand' and not directly under the law of love, gave a formal recognition to the 'shudder' which was lacking in other realist thinking. See *Secular Authority* I.4.

But Christian pacifists are more numerous than Christian anarchists. Many, perhaps most, of those who will not fight in a war, do not wish to discourage membership of a police force or office as a politician or judge. And here is the problem: this more sociable form of pacifism is vulnerable to the analogy between the judicial and military tasks. The similarites between the soldier and the magistrate offer a classic line of anti-pacifist polemic. If someone feels that war is so horrible that he must renounce it altogether, let him look realistically at the way in which states (all states!) maintain their order and stability. Police interrogation, riot control, long terms of imprisonment which disfigure the soul: all should produce the same revulsion. If he is consistent, let him either go the whole way to Mennonism and opt out of social control altogether, or let him learn to live with a queasy stomach. The pacifist position is made to appear unstable and inconsistent in its attitude to violence, capriciously objecting to violence between states, accepting violence within them.

In response to this challenge, the pacifist (who will be supposed, for the rest of our discussion, to approve of normal governmental activities) has only one line of defence. He must challenge the analogy between warfare and government; he must deny that war could count as a proper expression of governmental authority. He must show that the activities of the judge and the soldier are different, different enough to make any attempt to justify one by reference to the other impossible. This defence will bring him into head-on disagreement with the misleadingly-named 'Just War theory' of Christendom. The 'theory' (which might better be called 'Just War demand') is best understood as being two things at once: it is an interpretative proposal, that war should be understood as a kind of governmental administration of justice, and a moral demand, that its conduct should be regulated accordingly. The disagreement between the two positions thus turns decisively on the analogy between war and justice. It is this issue, together with possible moves towards a *rapprochement,* that I wish to explore.

2. VIOLENCE AND GOVERNMENT

The first point at which the pacifist may hope to drive his wedge between warfare and just government concerns their respective dependence on violence. If he can establish that war needs violence and just government does not, he is well on the way to carrying the case that war is not a legitimate act of government. Unfortunately, the claim that just government does not rely on violence is unlikely to gain much support, especially in our current sociologically-dominated climate of opinion which tends to be sceptical of governments.[1]

Rather than rely on the sociologists, however, it is worth our while to venture a brief sketch of a New Testament philosophy of government, demonstrating, as we may hope, that an idealistic conception of government-without-violence is inadequate not only empirically but theologically. Such a sketch will also provide a foundation for later developments in the discussion. It must, of course, be attempted with a certain caution. The New Testament writers should not be forced to give support for doctrines which never entered their minds (as has happened only too often in the course of Christian history, as different regimes have demanded theological backing). They have no views on what constitutes legitimacy in government, what institutions make for political justice, what the proper limits of civil obedience are, how the distribution of power should be effected, nor on many other questions like them. The very concept of 'the state' is unknown to the apostles, who speak sometimes of 'kings' (which is narrower) and sometimes of 'authorities' (which is broader). Nevertheless, we must not abandon the attempt as hopeless. Serious discussion about political authority is to be found in the New Testament, and, though limited, it is consistent and coherent.[2] Addressing themselves to the vexatious theological problem of how this world and its institutions relate to a radical eschatological hope, the apostles ask, 'Is there a place for one who accepts God's new order to obey those who assert their authority over him?', and reply, 'For the time being, yes.' For although 'the sons of the king' recognize an incongruity in their being taxed and tolled by the king's minor officials, they are content, for the moment, to preserve their *incognito* (Matt. 17.24ff.) And this, not only on the principle that submission is anyway a good thing (so that we love our enemies and pray for those that

1 Not every apologist for Christian pacifism will be prepared to make use of this argument; the philosophy of government developed here would command a fairly wide assent among pacifist writers, especially among those with a strong concern for Biblical integrity. For the purpose of this discussion, 'violence' and 'force' will be used as synonyms. As will appear, I do not agree that there is no point in distinguishing them, but to save begging the question I make no use of the distinction.

2 The key New Testament texts are: Mk. 12.13-17, Matt. 17.24ff., Rom. 13.1-6, 2 Thess. 2.6-8. But every bit as important are many texts which reflect an attitude to government incidentally: Lk. 13.32, 22.25ff., Jn. 18.36, 19.11, Acts 4.19 etc. And no study on the subject could afford to omit a careful reading of Revelation in its entirety.

The carefully balanced ambivalence in the New Testament witness is difficult to capture: some will stress the positive, some the negative aspects more decisively. In our survey the negative features may tend to predominate, if only to be sure that what we say can be said about *any* government, not merely about the good ones.

despitefully use us), but, more positively, actually recognizing that political authority, though not the final answer of a God who adopts men as his sons, nevertheless has divine authorization as a provisional arrangement for a world not yet redeemed.

(a) Divine Institution

Reflecting on this attitude, common both to the teaching of Jesus and St. Paul, we may observe that it is the nature of political authority not simply to be tolerated but to be acknowledged. This kind of relationship beween one man and another has a place in God's purposes. There is all the difference in the world between being locked up in a bedroom by a housebreaker and being locked up in a cell by a magistrate, undesirable as both experiences are and *unjust* as both may quite possibly be. I can contemplate with the greatest equanimity a world without housebreakers; I should not wish for a world without magistrates (though I may very well wish that the magistrates were better than they are), until the day when Christ assumes their office into his own. To speak of the *divine institution* of political authority is to say, what the 'social contract' myth says in other terms, that such authority actually does serve human needs. 'He is God's servant for your good' (Rom. 13.4). It is a necessary provision for any world in which there are housebreakers (even though a Christian, confronted with a housebreaker in his own home, may believe he should not resist him); but more than that, it would be necessary even in a world conforming to the Utopian dreams of earlier generations, where housebreakers had been educated out of existence—it would be necessary in any world where there were too few resources for too many appetites, where individuals were less than perfectly wise, perfectly impartial and perfectly informed. Finitude, as well as wickedness, demands that there shall be authority if we are to live comfortably together and not simply suffer at one another's hands. God has not left us to suffer. There is no place, then, for tortured despair about the realities of political power.[1]

(b) Justice

But any suggestion that 'divine authorization' offers the political authorities a *carte blanche* to make what demands they will, is countered by a second feature of the New Testament conception: the need that governments exist to meet is the need of *justice*, to execute God's wrath on the wrongdoer'. Justice is a moral state of affairs, and so the success and failure of governments has to be judged by moral criteria. Apologists for strong-arm regimes are fond of saying that government exists to maintain *order.* But this lets government get away too lightly. 'Justice' is a moral concept, 'order' is not. Because they measured government by moral standards (a concern they inherited from the Old Testament), the New Testament writers reckoned not only with the divine authorization of political activity but also with its tendency to degenerate into demonic oppression. There is, of course, a difference between the moral principles which govern the behaviour of an individual acting as a private person and those which govern his behaviour as a bearer of authority, the difference between 'love' and 'justice'. But even love and justice should not be

[1] Such as we find throughout Jacques Ellul's *Violence*, (S.C.M. London, 1970).

thought of as opposed and contradictory principles: justice is what the loving man seeks to achieve in performing the special tasks of political authority. To analyse the notion of justice is a complex and lengthy under-taking, and for our purposes it is enough simply to characterize it as 'impartiality', the disinclination to lean, in the use of one's power, either to one's own interest against another's or to the interests of a second party against those of a third.

In the Old and New Testament alike the paradigm of political activity is 'giving judgment': defending the rights of the weak plaintiff against the oppression of the strong. Government exists not to serve *every* interest of its people, but the specific interest that they all have in just arbitration. And yet 'justice' must not be interpreted too narrowly. To minds brought up on the doctrine of the 'separation of the powers' Paul's words about 'retribution on the offender' may suggest the activity of the courts, perhaps only the criminal courts at that, and appear to have no relevance to the 'executive' and 'legislative' branches of government. Such an idea would be very foreign to the ancient world. Justice was the concern of the king in any and all of his activities. All government is concerned with 'giving judgment', for all government is concerned with reconciling conflicting claims of different parties, with limiting the freedom of one to enhance the freedom of another; and so it touches on legislative and executive, as well as on judicial acts, that they should fulfil the moral purpose of govern-ment and 'have no terror for good behaviour'. Arbitrary and unjust acts can be performed by civil servants, ministers and parliamentarians no less than by policemen. In that they fail to arbitrate fairly between the rival claims of men or groups of men, they fail in their responsibility as holders of political authority.

(c) The Limits of the Age
However justly government may be conducted, there is a contradiction between Christianity and political relationships which cannot be escaped. 'In the world kings lord it over their subjects, and those in authority are called their country's "Benefactors". Not so with you.' (Lk. 22.25ff.). The exercise of power over other men's destinies is not one of the characteristic relationships of the sons of the Kingdom, where the highest bears himself like the youngest, the chief like a servant. Political authority is not part of that heavenly life to which Christ came to call men. Once upon a time in Israel's history it had been thought that power and authority could be without offence, that war might be waged, and the tasks of government performed, at the immediate promptings of the Spirit of God. This was the Mosaic ideal, the aspiration of the conquering community as it settled in the Promised Land; its failure and disappearance was attributed by the prophets of later Israel to the failure of the people to live consistently within the conditions laid down at Sinai. In rejecting the possibility within the historical order of such purified power and charismatic magistracy the New Testament has not turned its back entirely on the Holy War and allied concepts; rather, following the prophets, it has made them the basis for its understanding of the End, the final triumph of the Kingdom, when Christ shall reign as the new Moses, the new Joshua, the new David. To

expropriate the hopes and aspirations of Sinai to the governments of the nations would appear to be, not simply immoral (as modern liberalism might find it) but blasphemous.[1]

From the eschatological paradox of a Kingdom announced but not yet fully realised, we understand the moral paradox of the human kingdoms, recognized, but only with a shudder. It is important to realize that the shudder is not about *injustice* (except, perhaps, in a very relative sense). The scandal to the conscience when a magistrate destroys the life or prospects of another man could not be avoided in every case if only magistrates would judge more justly. Perhaps the Christian, looking at things from the divine point of view, will want to say with Augustine that the best that can be achieved is 'the unequal conventions of men'.[2] Perhaps, too, he will want to argue that the most perfect justice would also be perfectly loving, and that this is the message of the Atonement. True, but this message must not be sentimentalized by being shorn of its eschatological reference. Such a justice is God's justice, not man's. The miseries of long prison sentences, heavy fines, public disgrace, not to mention compulsory purchase orders, taxation, destruction of the environment and all the other necessary evils of organized government, could not always be avoided with just a little more time, trouble and thought. Better to face the fact that justice is a harsh and tragic virtue, belonging to an age which has not yet seen the wiping away of tears. The New Testament, naturally enough, supposes that believers are going to meet justice from the underside, such was the powerlessness of the earliest Christian community. It would be consistent, however, with its ambivalent welcome for the authority of others, that a believer, given the opportunity to wield authority himself,

---

[1] At the risk of serious over-generalization, we may say that this 'blasphemy' is a hallmark of much recent 'Liberation' theology, inasmuch as it appropriates freely the categories of Exodus, Sinai and Conquest, and invokes them on behalf of modern political groupings in their struggle for social justice. (So did the Scottish Covenanters, the Tsars, and many other heirs of the Holy War tradition). John H. Yoder's claim (*Karl Barth and the Problem of War* (Abingdon Press, Nashville Tenn, 1970) p.14) that 'the more recent call for a "theology of revolution" simply repeats the logic of the classical "just war" tradition with the roles reversed' is very wide of the mark. Just War thinking begins, as does pacifism, by treating Jesus' refusal of the sword in the Garden of Gethsemane as normative (Matt. 27.51-54). Ideological or religious wars are rejected: war is only contemplated within the limits of secular judicial administration. Barth may have misled Yoder here: his concessions to war, though limited, are more typical of the Holy War than of the Just War tradition.

Yet we cannot simply record a negative judgment on the Liberation Theology movement. It represents a healthy and overdue scepticism towards the romantic Western Christianity which has had no place for the virtue of justice, whether human or divine. Can we be surprised that when we have attempted, for more than a century, to erase the judgment of God from our theological thinking, it persistently erupts back again in a series of theological reactions that seem harsh simply because they represent something about Christianity that we badly need and yet are ashamed of? All we can say to this and other zealot movements in the church, is that they must reckon on the difference between the divine and eschatological and the human and provisional. Even Christian revolutionaries must be humble about their achievements!

[2] *City of God* XIX.21.

would take it, but with a sinking feeling in his stomach. The logic of New Testament eschatology leads us back to the attitudes of Socrates.[1]

(d) The Powers that Exist

Bearers of political authority are necessarily publicly identifiable. When we ask, 'To whom, then, do we defer in this reserved, but essentially constructive, way?' the answer is given, 'To the existing authorities' (Rom. 13.1), i.e. the representatives of institutionalized power as we see it around us at the moment. We are not entitled to reserve the appellation 'government' grudgingly in our bosom until at last someone appears who seems worthy of it. In most circumstances political power institutionalizes itself according to some pattern of publicly recognizable authority. 'The state', as we know it, is one such institutionalization, but there is no theological presumption in favour of nation-states rather than (say) village headmen. The reality of political authority is the same in either case.

This *de facto* basis for governmental authority is offensive to idealists of all persuasions, those who believe that no government is a government unless it is democratically elected, or unless it serves some egalitarian end, or unless it is run by the linear descendent of the person who used to run it, or unless the racial background of the governors and the governed is the same. Any or all of these factors may be important in deciding whether a government can succeed; but to make them conditions for its legitimacy is a mistake. The legitimation of a government depends on what we loosely call 'effective control', which is to say that the one who has a right to be recognized is the one who is actually exercising authority. It may be desirable that he should hand over control to someone else, or that he should exercise it in a different way; and it may make perfect sense to demand either of these things. But it makes no sense to say that he is not the government when he obviously is. Nothing is served by theories of legitimacy which deny that facts are as they are.

Two factors make for effective control: one is force, so that authority can effectively 'give judgment' against the oppressor, who may be expected to resist; the other is the general acceptance of those who are governed. All governments rest on these two supports in different proportions. Some need a very great measure of force because they have little consent; but even they can continue to exist only through a degree of passive resignation. Others require comparatively little force since they have a lot of consent (not necessarily because they are *popular,* but because they can count on the general co-operation of the public in routine duties); but even they need enough force to arrest violent criminals and to enforce the orders of the courts. There is, then, a certain one-sided truth in the sociologists' observation that government is institutionalized violence, a truth which has its recognition in the New Testament ('It is not for nothing that he carries the sword' (Rom. 13.4)), and which has been the common theme of Christian 'realists' from Augustine to Reinhold Niebuhr. The reason that governments cannot function without violence is that the task God has given them is to

---

[1] With this difference, however: whereas Socrates' wise man accepted responsibility because he could discharge it well, but reluctantly because it was tedious and unimportant to him; the Christian is reluctant to bear responsibility because neither he nor anyone else can do it well, but does so because it is important.

control violent men. Of course, a government quickly loses respect if it resorts too hastily to drastic measures, for it is part of the art of government to use the minimum force necessary; but it would lose all claim to be the government at all if it renounced the use of force entirely. We might define a government as: that institution in a community which is generally recognized to have the right to use force when all else fails.

If pacifism depends on the claim that governments can do without violence, it is liable to turn back into anarchism after all. However, although it is possible to be naive about the use of force in government, imagining that everything can be done by consent and co-operation, it is possible, too, to be cynical. It is not for nothing, after all, that the violence of governments is *institutionalized*, and thereby controlled. When realists join forces with anarchists to argue, half-quoting Augustine, that since the best-run state is nothing but 'a great gang of terrorists', there can be nothing to choose between 'force' as exercised by governments and 'violence' as exercised by terrorists, it will not do. It is one thing to give money to Robin Hood, another to give it to the Sheriff of Nottingham. Regardless of which demands it more politely, which makes the louder threats, which will use it better, the Sheriff is the Sheriff. He can tax us, while Robin Hood can only hold us at bowpoint and request a contribution for an Irish charity. The commonplace observation that all regimes began as revolutions is perfectly true; but the point is, they are not *now* revolutions. A political authority claims the right to do the very things which individuals and private groups are forbidden to do. But then, if government is to be good for mankind, you cannot have two rival governments in one place. Those who live in an area where the Sheriff of Nottingham collects taxes by day while Robin Hood, calling himself the Sheriff of Nottingham, collects taxes by night, each powerless to prevent the other, are unhappy indeed. It is they who will appreciate best that settled government is a blessing of God and will prefer to live under one real regime, indifferent though its achievement may be, than under two conflicting claimants. The difference between force and violence is not what is done, but who does it: and that is not a cynical observation, because it *does matter* that only one group of people, and they reasonably well co-ordinated, should pretend to do this kind of thing in any one community at any one time. These observations are not meant to constitute an argument against revolution. They merely insist that revolution is one thing, settled government another, and that, whether or not the former may be justifiable *in extremis,* it is the latter that God has given us as a severe blessing for our mediocre world. Government is good for people in a nasty sort of way. The government that *exists* must be recognized, damn it!

3. JUSTICE AND WAR

The 'Just War Theory' of mediaeval and renaissance Christendom represented a systematic attempt to interpret acts of war by analogy with acts of civil government, not, be it noted, to afford some *justification* for warmaking, but to bring it under the *restraint* of those moral standards which apply to other acts of government. It is a limiting doctrine. It rejects the old philosophy that 'All's fair in love and war' (at least with respect to the second), and declares that if political authority expects to fight wars in discharge of its responsibilities, it shall be expected in turn to fight them *justly*. But what is it to fight wars 'justly'? The Just War tradition singled out five principles: First, that the authority responsible for waging war should actually be a 'magistrate', that is, should bear responsibility for civil justice in some community. Secondly, that the *cause* should be just, an obvious, but perhaps not otiose, stipulation. Thirdly, examining the complexities of human motivation, and recognizing that it is possible to perform just deeds for a whole range of corrupt reasons, it added that the *motive* should be just too. The fourth and fifth criteria concerned the manner in which war, once begun, should be conducted. The principle of *discrimination* demanded that only those who were themselves in arms should be made the object of direct armed attack. While attempting to defeat the force brought against his own community, the magistrate would respect the fabric of the enemy community, and even protect it. The purpose of government is to achieve justice, and justice is never achieved by indiscriminate acts. The principle of *proportion*, finally, demanded that only such measures as were actually necessary to secure a stable peace should be taken. 'Overkill' is as much an offence against justice as is killing indiscriminately.

A full exposition of this theory lies beyond the scope of our discussion, and I have gone even into such meagre detail as this only because of an uncomfortable suspicion that many who loosely criticise 'just war', from a militarist as well as from a pacifist point of view, are unfamiliar with it. Its historical origins are not important for our purposes.[1] It matters only because it presents the case which pacifism must meet. Much pacifist argument is content to score cheaply by stalking easy game such as the uncritical militarism which would free the practice of war from any moral restraint. The Just War theory plainly intends to treat moral considerations very seriously; it claims to report what a sense of natural justice self-evidently demands in acts of war. In this respect the second and third canons are almost tautologous, while the fourth and fifth, which form the real cutting-edge of the theory as a programme for restraint, bear a close relationship to the natural justice of the courts: just as a judge sentences only those who are guilty, not others who may be related to them or live near them, and only with a punishment proportionate to what they have done, not on all occasions with the maximum penalty possible; so the magistrate at war makes direct acts of hostility only against those who are acting with direct hostility, not against their uncles and cousins, and only with such force as is necessary to defeat the threat, not with the maximum force he can deploy.[2]

[1] On the evolution of the theory, see Sydney D. Bailey, *Prohibitions and Restraints In War* (Royal Institute of International Affairs and O.U.P., 1972) pp.1-57.

[2] The principle of discrimination allows, of course, for *unintended* non-combatant casualties.

The first canon attempts to define the analogy, stipulating that warfare may take place only in the context of the administration of justice. Only he who anyway bears responsibility within the community for defending the rights of the weak against the strong, only he, and acting only in that capacity, may take responsibility for defending those rights against oppression from outside. This principle is not, or need not be, a prohibition of revolution, provided only that the responsibility for administering justice is indivisible, and that the revolutionary, as self-appointed magistrate, accepts the obligation to provide justice impartially and effectively for *any* member of the community he attempts to control. The immoral revolution and the immoral war are entirely alike, in that they fail to see the organic connexion between warfare and justice, and so subordinate justice to winning.

Any government that embarks upon a war feels the need of moral support among its people, and tries to secure it by intensive propaganda. But the more it succeeds in whipping up war-enthusiasm, the more danger there is that the model may be lost sight of: instead of being an act of executive justice, war is presented, and thought about, as an act of popular feeling. The model presumes that anybody who acts in an executive capacity, whether as common soldier, general, War Minister or President, acts to defend the just claims of *others*. But the matter is easily presented as though a collective entity, 'the people' or 'the nation', is acting to defend *itself.* And when everybody thinks about it this way, this, in a sense, is what is happening. The Just War theory has often been presented in this form, as a justification for collective self-defence. Critics arguing from a pacifist point of view are quick to point out that self-defence is forbidden by Christ (Matt. 6.39-48), and to accuse the theory of a double standard, one rule for the individual, another for the collective.[1] But in its original Augustinian form the theory made no use of a supposed right of collective self-defence. Such a 'right' would not only disregard the prohibitions of the Sermon on the Mount, but would obscure the basic concept of the theory which is to interpret war as an act of responsible magistracy.[2] A spirit of collective self-defence, however useful to the politicians, is hardly a judicial spirit; it is more likely to inflame all kinds of nationalist fanaticisms. Christ's prohibition of self-defence can be respected as binding on individuals and collectives alike. The defence of others is what in question, individuals and collectives alike. The defence of others is what is in question, and that not randomly, in a swashbuckling Good Samaritan spirit, but under the restraining standards of executive justice.[3]

[1] Thus Christopher Sugden, in an earlier contribution to this series, criticises Paul Ramsey for distinguishing 'personal ethics, in which non-resistance is the norm, and social ethics, where one ought to resist on another's behalf', and adds: 'Respectable theological tradition, stemming from Luther's Two Kingdoms theory, has understood the sermon on the mount in this way.' (*A Different Dream*, p.17). In fact the passage he quotes from Ramsey's *Basic Christian Ethics* says nothing about a distinction between personal and social ethics. It only distinguishes 'the simplest moral situation' from 'the more complex cases when non-resistance would in practice mean turning from another person's face to the blows of an oppressor'. The moral norms are the same either way: it is *the kind of case* which is different. This is a far cry from the double-standard of the Two Kingdoms theory.

[2] Augustine does not believe in a right of self-defence (*On Free Will* I.5.12); St. Thomas Aquinas does (*S.T.* II-II.64.7).

[3] See note at foot of p.15 opposite.

4. THE ANALOGY UNDER ATTACK

But when important distinctions are overlooked, moral thinking goes awry. If the state is really just another gang of terrorists, the only options left to us seem to be total withdrawal from political activity or the wholesale abandonment of our moral scruples; but it is not. What, then, if good government is just another act of war? Notwithstanding all that we have said about government's dependence on force, this question ought to make us feel uncomfortable. Just as it is one thing to be taxed by the Sheriff of Nottingham and another to be robbed by Robin Hood, so it is one thing to be thrown in jail for one's alleged crimes and another to be cooped up in a P.O.W. camp, one thing to be hanged at the order of a court, another to be blown to smithereens by a landmine. The analogy is an analogy and no more, and there are differences to explore as well as similarities. The pacifist will want to press these differences home. Warfare, he will say, cannot be just another case of 'giving judgment'; for the virtue of human judgment is justice, and since war cannot be conformed to the minimal demands of justice as we naturally understand it, either it is not judgment at all, or it is a kind of judgment that is intrinsically immoral. Either way the Just War enterprise falls down. This case can be developed rather forcefully.

(a) Third-Party Arbitration
It is clear that bilateral warfare cannot be disinterested and impartial. It is conceivable, perhaps, that in *multilateral* situations an impartial war could be waged. In Northern Ireland the British army, representing the recognized government, has the task of keeping the peace impartially between two partly-armed communities. In principle this impartiality is thought to be attainable, however difficult it may be to achieve in practice. In the same way one might imagine a third force intervening *outside* its area of responsibility, in order to hold two warring parties apart, and we can even imagine a situation in which such an intervention would be welcomed by both sides. A third party is not necessarily disinterested, of course, but it may be: international peace-keeping forces, such as are occasionally sent by the United Nations, act on this assumption and with this intention. But if disinterested warfare cannot be ruled out *a priori* in a triangular or multilateral situation, in the more normal form of war, where the forces are polarized, it can. (And we may want to add that all our experience of 'international peace-keeping' suggests that as soon as such an impartial force actually *acts,* it is seen to support one side or the other so that the conflict is once again polarized). Certainly, nations may sometimes claim

---

Note 3 of p.14 opposite
  John H. Yoder, ' "What Would You Do If . . . ?" ' in *Journal of Religious Ethics,* 1974, pp.81-105, argues quite rightly against the paradigm case of someone shooting to defend his wife or child from an assailant. In a family, as he points out, there is a 'community of choice', the possibility for a shared decision of self-sacrifice. I can hardly accuse Dr. Yoder of 'stalking easy game' since the family-paradigm is all too popular in Christian realist argument. But the nation is *not* a family—as Augustine, though (again) not Aquinas, was well aware. It would be much more telling to imagine the headmaster of an infants' school in the same situation. But this, too, is inadequate: the only paradigm in which the Just War theory is really interested is that of the policeman or judge.

to wage war out of distinterested concern for the world in general, and such claims may be sincere. But they cannot be true. Their perceptions of what is in the world's best interests are coloured by their own points of view. Such perceptions, no less than the frankly seflish pursuit of private interests, may lead to conflict. True judgment must be able to arbitrate, not only between conflicts of selfishness but between conflicts of high-mindedness.

If a government, concerned to provide justice for its people, finds that it cannot do so unless it takes up arms against an external aggressor, then it steps out of the role of judge *between* parties into the role of advocate *for* a party. Hitherto it has tried to ensure that one person's or group's interests do not constantly prevail over another's; but in so doing it has been responsible for the interests of both. Precisely because it does not stand in the same mediatorial relation between its own people and their enemies, it cannot provide justice between nations. This only a third party could do. In a dispute between the linen manufacturers of Lancashire and the (British) importers of Pakistani linen, the British government owns a duty to protect the rights of both manufacturers and importers, and so can arbitrate between them. But in a dispute between the Lancashire manu-facturers and the Pakistani manufacturers, the British government, responsible for only one of the parties' interests, could not be unbiassed.

(b) Legitimacy
But even if a warring power were to guarantee the even-handed adminis-tration of justice for the enemy community, one essential factor would still be lacking. To exercise political authority, it would need consent. It would have to be recognized as the government by the community it pretended to govern. Powers which christen their conquests 'wars of liberation' are all too well aware that the legitimacy of a conquest depends on its being welcome to the vanquished. But in fact few communities will welcome conquest by an alien power (though there may be an occasional exception in the extreme case, such as at the fall of Nazi Germany). To be legitimate, judgment must be acceptable—not, perhaps, in the strong sense that all parties are prepared to accept each particular decision, but at least in the weaker sense that all parties accept the decisions of that authority in general. And so any act of war will lack an essential constituent of legitimacy.

(c) Practicality
But even these objections have allowed, for the sake of argument, that a government really *can* act in a judicial spirit in the conduct of war. Experi-ence teaches us, however, that such an approach to warfare exists only in the text-books of morality. The popular concept of war as collective self-defence may be repudiated by moral theologians, but it is actually a psychological inevitability. Just War theory demands that war should be conducted in a frame of mind that everybody knows to be impossible. War *will* encourage the collectivist fanaticism which the theorists deplore. It *will* be seen as a struggle for 'our' homes, 'our' children, 'our' future; and the more it requires the total participation of society in the war-effort, the more inevitable this understanding becomes. Thus 'justice' in war is unobtainable. Pacifist apologists, it may be said, in addressing themselves

to the concept of war as national self-defence, address themselves to the reality; and perhaps they may be pardoned for ignoring a case so utterly academic as that which the Just War theory offers!

The Response

A response to these arguments must examine more attentively what is meant when we describe an action as 'just'. Let us propose: an action may be called 'just' if it arbitrates between two causes entirely fairly, accurately assessing the relative claims of each, discerning all the factors which affect the case, resolving on a course of action which rectifies all imbalances without creating new ones. True enough, no doubt, but such an action is never performed in real life! If we insist on thinking of justice in purely quantified terms, as the art of dividing £10 equally among four men, then, certainly, we will not understand why any action should not be perfectly just: £2·50 is the right sum for each, and any deviation, even of a penny, is unjust and unnecessary. But suppose that the £10 is meant to pay the four men for their work: can we be sure that A did not work harder than B? and can we quantify the difference precisely if he did? Or suppose that it is meant to support them in their need: do we not suspect that C has greater needs than D? and how do we express the liability of an invalid grandmother as a fraction of £10? In life-situations our attempts at justice will be rough. The all-sublime object of Gilbert's Mikado, to make the punishment fit the crime, is all too sublime for the actual powers of human discernment. We deal in approximations, and the deeper we examine situations the more we despair of knowing what justice demands. No law designed to remedy an injustice ever failed to create a new one. No action to protect the interests of these men ever failed to ride roughshod over the interests of those. Justice is not to be measured by an absolute standard: in human dealings (whatever we may say about God's final assize) it is a relative matter, a question of more or less.

(a) Third-Party Arbitration

In the formal administration of civil and criminal justice, third-party arbitration is a normal procedural rule. The reasons for adopting such a rule are obvious enough; the third party transcends, not merely the selfishness of the interested parties but their limitations of perspective, their unconscious injustices as well as their malicious ones. Yet even a perfectly scrupulous third party cannot achieve anything absolute; and there may be times when the third party, because he is not himself involved in the dispute, is insensitive to serious considerations which touch the participants. (Which is why a judicial system needs not only judges but advocates: judges cannot be trusted to see all the issues without help). So the procedural rule of third-party arbitration, though a device of the greatest importance, must not be thought an indispensable criterion for calling any settlement 'just'. This is quite obvious when we look from the more formal examples to the informal. An argument about (let us say) a fair rent will only be referred for arbitration if the parties are unable to agree between themselves on what is fair. It would be absurd to say that no rent could be fair that had not been laid down by a tribunal. Rather, we assume that a rent is fair unless one of the parties complains, because the very fact of agreement argues (in normal market conditions, between equally-matched participants) that the settled sum is a just one. And indeed not only is justice possible in a bilateral situation. Even when one party unilaterally can lay down terms to another, it is conceivable that he may be scrupulous enough to lay down fair terms. Of course, there is no guarantee that he will, and no guarantee that he will have a very balanced assessment of what is fair (which is why monopolies and compulsory purchase orders are always suspect in practice); but he may. The point is simply that the categories of more and less fair are still applicable. I can say, 'That is not a fair price for my house'; but I wait until I have seen the price before I say it, and do not know automatically, from the mere fact that it is imposed by a compulsory purchase order, that it is unfair by definition.

And so we can still ask, of any action undertaken by a warring power, 'Is it just?', without knowing in advance that the answer must be 'No'. Certainly it is a great disadvantage to justice that third-party arbitration is difficult to impose on international hostilities. But in itself this does not make the concept of international justice empty. The pacifist comes dangerously near to saying that there can be no international justice at all. In fact nations do try, though not always very hard, to regulate international affairs justly; and the effect of such a counsel would simply be that they ceased trying. There is one significant force which acts as informal arbitrator and restrainer: world opinion. Nations who depend on easy trading contracts are modestly sensitive to the bad opinion of their trading partners; and although this is not an entirely effective constraint, (for nations do, frequently, behave very badly), it demonstrates that there is an idea of international justice, which is hard for any nation to disown, waiting to be developed and given a more formal embodiment through world institutions.

(b) Legitimacy

International opinion goes some way, too, towards solving the difficulty about legitimacy. Assuming, as seems reasonable, that any people who are the object of an alien government's officious intervention will resent it, and that no invaded community is likely to regard the invading troops as 'legitimate' arbitrators in their affairs, this, nevertheless, does not mean that legitimacy is always impossible in war. It is no condition of legitimacy in judicial matters that a magistrate should be *invited* to arbitrate a case. No doubt the party against whom judgment falls usually resents the interference of the law; and in some cases accused make great play of 'refusing to recognize the court'. But that is neither here nor there: the question is whether an authority is *generally* recognized to have the right to arbitrate. And in international disputes the question is whether the international community *in general* acknowledges the legitimacy of a nation's armed involvement. For, despite pious politicians' talk about abhorring violence wherever it occurs, the international community is plainly inclined to make distinctions. It did not approve of what American troops were doing in Vietnam, but it does approve of what they do in Germany. Of course it may be highly misguided and capricious in either of these judgments, or in any other. The point is not that world opinion is infallibly just, nor even that it offers an adequate procedure for assessing justice in international affairs. But it does suggest that a procedure could be developed, through the

United Nations or in some other way; and it demonstrates that the concept of legitimate war, though as yet without any stable criteria, is as least not senseless.

(c) Practicality
The impossibility of just war, of which the pacifist complains, is as relative a matter as justice itself. There are more just and less just wars, more just and less just actions within war, more just and less just attitudes among communities engaged upon war, (and the theory, it must be remembered, is concerned with all three of these matters and not only with the first). There would be no point in claiming that there has ever been a perfectly just war; but then moral theory as a whole does not claim that there has ever been a perfectly just man. It is enough to say simply that we have a *duty* to do the more, rather than the less, just thing, to hold the more, rather than the less, just attitude. Human nature being what it is, a majority of any people at war is likely to develop immoral attitudes towards their enterprise; but that is no reason why any individual should allow himself to do so, and no reason why our moral educators should not encourage us to think responsibly and dispassionately. And it is no reason in particular why statesmen should not forcefully be told what morality demands of them, 'whether they hear or whether they forbear'. Experience suggests that they usually forbear; but in this matter the Just War theorist and the pacifist are in the same boat, for both believe in standards of right and wrong of which they are unlikely to persuade either the population or its statesmen.

Where the Just War theorist and the pacifist differ is over the question whether the justice of an act of war is determined, in isolation from other issues, simply by virtue of the fact that it is war. For the pacifist the word 'war', like the word 'fornication', is already the name of a sin. For his opponent it is more like the term 'intercourse', which leaves the moral question open. He doubts whether any given act of war can be evaluated in isolation from its context, the search for justice in international relations. War stands to the web of international arbitration as the magistrate's sword stands to the web of government. To ask whether war can be just is like asking whether execution can be just: everything depends on what has gone before it, and what the other possibilities are. Just War theory defends war only as the ultimate recourse which legitimates, and makes possible, the non-violent administration of justice between nations. To pacifism it returns the question: what are we to do about international justice if we renounce the ultimate possibility of force? And it is, I believe, as they consider that question together that the two contenders will discover a considerable territory of thought opening up before them which they may hold in common.

5. INTERNATIONAL JUSTICE: SOME COMMON GROUND

1. Non-Lethal Sanctions

First of all the pacifist may ask, using to his own purpose the analogy which has been used so relentlessly against him, whether there is no equivalent in international justice to the abolition of the death penalty. Justice in communities is held to rest upon the ultimate sanction of the magistrate's sword, but this does not mean that he uses the sword on every occasion, nor even that he threatens to. The possession of the sword makes possible a carefully graduated series of non-lethal constraints, and the greater the co-operation from the public the less likelihood is there that these will be exhausted. The state is very rarely forced to shoot from the hip. It has sanctions short of imprisonment, it has prisons of various grades, and to cope with jail-breaks it has bloodhounds and a highly co-ordinated detection service. Remote and unpredictable indeed is the chain of events that leads from the magistrate's court to the arbitration of the slug. Since, then, the tide of communal order can rise high enough to float the penal system semi-autonomously off its support of violence, cannot international justice function in the same way, and develop intermediate, non-lethal sanctions?[1]

The answer, we must hope, is that there is no reason why it should not. But hitherto non-lethal sanctions have been difficult to develop. Opinion will be divided on whether Rhodesia was brought to terms primarily by economic sanctions or by the growth of guerilla violence; but either way it is unlikely that sanctions without violence could have achieved more than they had achieved in ten indecisive years. Their failure was a great disappointment, not only to those who wanted to see a change of regime in Rhodesia, but to those who wanted to make international coercion work without killing people. Failing economic weapons, the world has had to rely on a series of ever more developed and formalized diplomatic gestures, which serve to pass judgment without actually invoking execution. Small public affronts, such as the breaking of diplomatic relations or exclusion from the Olympic Games, provide means short of violence for administering retribution on errant nations. Realists may find such gestures amusing, sportsmen may find them distasteful. But neither derision nor irritation is appropriate. Punishment is a bit like paper money, effective so long as it is generally believed in; it is all in our interests that such measures should be believed in. Britain's 'cod wars' with Iceland deserve some attention in this context. History may decide that they represent a major step for civilization by pioneering a method of hostilities which works entirely by inflicting minor damage on property. Once again, the main requirement is that both sides should believe this kind of dispute really damages them. The trawlermen of Hull saw to that, by reacting to their periodic battles of net-slashing with a histrionic relish which would have done credit to history's greatest fighting forces.

---

[1] Paul Ramsey has written on the possible uses of non-lethal incapacitating gases, *The Just War* pp.465-478. It may be that our observations on the semi-autonomy of political order from violence would produce a hollow laugh in other societies than our own, in the U.S.A. for example. British readers ought to reflect on the reasons for this: it is not necessarily simply that foreigners are incompetent! Such freedom from violence as society can attain is extremely hard-won and very fragile.

However, there is a great distance to go before we can be certain of imposing settlements in international disputes without killing people. When we can, the Just War theory, by virtue of its principle of proportionate means, will agree with pacifism in demanding that only such non-lethal methods may be used.

2. Institutions for Arbitration

The second possibility for the administration of international justice is to insist on the third-party principle. If the right to use force was restricted to internationally authorized peace-keeping forces, then the pacifist might be persuaded to accept it as a genuine case of international government, while the Just War theorist would welcome it as a device to strengthen the likelihood of impartiality. But such forces would have to be at the disposal of international institutions which commanded some credibility as forms of world government. Such institutions exist in embryo, of course, in the United Nations and the World Court; but their present weaknesses give some ground for doubt as to whether the concept of international government is a realistic one. We must ask whether one of the strengths of effective governments is not precisely that they embody their community's sense of corporate identity *over against* other peoples. The slow development of a United Europe which we witness at present is an example of this: French, Danish and Irish all have an increasing sense of their common interests over against the large blocs of America, Africa and Asia. A United Europe will gain its cohesion from those it excludes, and so is more likely to be a step away from, rather than a step towards, a United World. No one can tell whether anything short of interplanetary warfare could produce the global solidarity which strong world-governmental institutions would presuppose. Nevertheless, these institutions are certainly worth trying to strengthen. International peace-keeping forces have already played a major part in securing international justice, and represent an important step towards taming the horrors of bilateral warfare. We must neither exaggerate their possibilities nor deny them.

3. Abandoning the Cause

Nevertheless, it is still all too possible that a nation may be forced into a conflict which no third party can arbitrate. And so we consider another possibility, a radical suggestion from the pacifist side, that at a certain point governments should abandon altogether the quest for macrocosmic justice and leave such matters to God, confining their attention to the task of establishing justice within the more manageable units entrusted to them. This is the clearest way of presenting a common pacifist demand, that the collective Christian duty of communities facing aggression is the path of non-resistance and suffering.

Most Christian thinkers will accept at its face-value Jesus' command that we should suffer rather than to resist those who oppress us. But just because this is a very difficult duty to fulfil personally, there is a particular embarrassment in recommending it collectively when one is oneself not in the most exposed position. If an American pacifist had said in 1940: 'Let us not resist, but rather suffer', he could only have meant, 'Let us not defend the Europeans, but let *them* suffer'. As Swift wrote, 'when *we* are lashed, *they* kiss the rod'. However, if we put the proposal in the tough-minded form, 'Let us not defend each other's just causes to the point of war, but rather entrust them to God', there is a good deal to be said for it:

(*a*) Morally, it might be argued that if submission really is a virtue and a duty, then we ought to encourage one another to practise it. The duty of suffering rather than resisting becomes a very easy option when accompanied by a mutual defence pact.

(*b*) Practically, failing the strong international institutions which we discussed above, any attempt to administer justice on an international scale may prove disproportionately hurtful. We never know in advance how long hostilities will last and to what degree of intensity they will blaze. Once they have begun, it is extremely difficult to prevent them from escalating into all-out war, and all-out war will leave nobody better off. It is better not to put one's hand to this perilous business at all. All human justice is something of a compromise, and there comes a point when one should pursue one's cause no further.

(*c*) Moreover the lives of men in their daily avocations are not so drastically affected by international injustice as they are by local injustice. Oppression at close quarters may do more to harm individuals than injustice between nations ever could. A Kashmiri farmer is more vulnerable to the ambitions of a neighbouring farmer than he is to the passage of his land from one nation's control to another's. But the worst of all eventualities would be that India and Pakistan should choose his fields on which to arbitrate their battle for his rights!

The Just War theorist can recognize in this proposal his own principle of proportionate means developed to a more radical degree. It is essential to the spirit of the Just War theory—and it is this that distinguishes it from conventional justifications of defence—that in the search for justice through armed conflict there is a cut-off point. One is not to resist *at any cost.* There are methods of war which it were better to be defeated than to use. A war which destroys the community whose cause it defends cannot be right; the quest for justice has to be abandoned somewhere. The principle which motivates the pacifist argument is thus actually written into his opponent's concept of justice. And it is this principle which brings both pacifist and Just War theorist alike into conflict with the conventional wisdom of deterrence, that the ultimate sanction has to be indefinitely credible if it is to provide the security for other means of arbitration to be used. Deterrence-theory is based on the premiss that an enemy will not share our belief that some prices are not worth paying for victory; and so the only form of sanction that can deter him is one that will guarantee his defeat. But this premiss is highly improbable. Enemy powers too have some sense of the cost of warfare, and some disinclination to pay it. The deterrent can deter as soon as it becomes unpleasantly costly to beat—and in most disputes (at least between moderately wealthy nations) that point is reached as soon as violent conflict comes in view. Naturally, the lower the scale of the ultimate sanction, the less secure the peace that it guarantees. But peace does not have to be 'absolutely' secure, only secure *enough.* And just as security can be enhanced by elaborating the lower-scale sanctions, so it can be shaken by expanding the higher-scale ones. The arms race itself, when it reaches a certain point, becomes an unsettling and threatening factor, a possible *casus belli*.

In all this the pacifist and Just War theorist can agree. The disagreement can be pinned down to the question of where the cut-off point comes. For the pacifist it comes where hostilities are prosecuted with lethal methods. For the 'nuclear pacifist' it comes when recourse is made to a much more dangerous and disproportionate form of weapon. The Just War theorist differs from both in hesitating to determine the point of disproportion in general terms. He is more uncertain in his expectations, not professing to know how terrible a threat to justice might present itself and what price might be reasonable to avert it. Against the pure pacifist he would argue that the agonies of war are not always worse for individuals than the collective shame of international injustice. International injustice does not always leave the ordinary citizen comparatively unaffected. Probably for the Kashmiri farmer it would be so, but for the Poles buried at Katyn it was not so. Those who fled to Britain from the gas-chambers of the Third Reich were actually saved because Britain resisted. On the whole it is hard to see how in the case of the Second World War justice could have been better served by non-resistance. Nevertheless, while hesitating to declare that the pursuit of justice by warfare can never be anything but self-defeating, and hesitating to declare that there could never be any use for a nuclear weapon in pursuit of a proportionate end, it is obvious enough to the Just War theorist that some weapons could have no conceivable use in the proportionate pursuit of anything, and that the attitude of preparing for the worst can be (in itself, and without actual hostilities) immoral. If nothing in our experience or imagination can justify the devastation of multi-megaton explosives with all their terrible destructiveness, why continue to brandish them? Just Warriors and pacifists alike will wish to address Western society with the urgent question: 'Is your weapon really necessary?'

APPENDIX: CHRISTOPHER SUGDEN ON NON-VIOLENT RESISTANCE

In an earlier contribution to this series, *A Different Dream—Non-Violence as Practical Politics*, Christopher Sugden, pleading that Christians should make non-violent methods their normal expression of resistance, makes some criticisms of Just War theory. This note briefly outlines where I can agree with him and where I believe we differ.

Most of the examples of non-violent resistance that interest Sugden are of organized protest against internal civil oppression. They present an alternative, not to war, but to civil strife or armed insurrection. The situation envisaged is one in which a state is evidently defective in the administration of justice, either through weakness, so that the strong oppress the weak without difficulty, or through partiality, so that the state itself is pppressive. Sugden does not claim that non-violence will always be 'practical politics' in this situation: sometimes it will work, sometimes it will not. The point is, that it will work rather more than we normally give it credit for, and that we should not feel ourselves forced to choose between disinvolvement and violence simply because there are no intermediate means at our disposal.

If non-violent resistance fails, of course, the cut-off point has been reached: we are content to suffer.

In this thesis we must admire the degree to which the author has avoided false and distorting antitheses. His state is not *either* just and unproblematic *or* unjust and therefore not a real state at all (as so often in the fairy-tale stories of the rhetoricians). His state is the state that we all actually know from experience, modestly successful in its task but yet with gaping holes in its fabric of justice, neither all-bad nor all-good. His non-violent resistance is neither a panacea nor a fruitless gesture. It can achieve just so much in certain favourable conditions. His case is certainly (to use his own term) 'chastened', if by that we mean that he has his feet on the ground.

It will be clear from our concluding section that we are sympathetic to any proposals for intermediate and non-lethal hostility. By the principle of proportion even a frank advocate of Just Revolution would have to say that where non-violent resistance could be effective in remedying injustice, no stronger methods should be used. We might sum up the case on which a Just War theorist could be brought to agree with Sugden in four propositions (I reserve judgment on the fourth):

(1) The government has a *prima facie* right to be obeyed, a right to use arms itself in case of need, and a right to forbid its citizens to use arms either against itself or against each other.

(2) Christians have a duty to show love to all men, including the oppressive.

(3) Christians have a particular duty to show practical love to the oppressed, and to speak frankly about injustice.

(4) The only way to fulfil all these three commitments in the event of civil oppression is the way of non-violent resistance.

The issue between Sugden and myself about war, then, is not actually central to his thesis. If he accepted the principles of the Just War theory, nothing of major significance in his position would have to be revised. However, he does not accept that war can be justified, but distinguishes, with arguments similar to (*a*) and (*b*) on p.17ff above, the justifiable violence required to maintain civil order within the state from the unjustifiable violence directed outside in war. In support of these arguments he appears to lean very heavily on the idea of consent as constituting legitimacy, and may even be taken to say at one point that states do not impose unwelcome and unpopular laws (p.11). 'The coercing body, the police, do not coerce the public to accept laws, only to obey laws that have been accepted.' (This is not supposed to be a description of a democracy, but of any state!) To which I reply, as Augustine did to Cicero, 'Then there never was a Roman republic!' Not even the best-run states correspond to these demanding specifications. I find it interesting that at this particular point in his argument Sugden has been drawn away from the more realistic model of the state that underlies his main thesis.